Tonics
& Teas

Traditional and modern remedies
that make you feel amazing

Rachel de Thample

Photography by Ali Allen

Kyle Books

First published in Great Britain in 2017 by
Kyle Books, an imprint of Kyle Cathie Ltd.
192–198 Vauxhall Bridge Road
London SW1V 1DX
general.enquiries@kylebooks.com
www.kylebooks.co.uk

10 9 8 7 6 5 4 3 2 1

ISBN 978 0 85783 444 7

Editor: **Hannah Coughlin**
Copy Editor: **Anne McDowall**
Designer: **Lucy Gowans**
Photographer and prop stylist: **Ali Allen**
Illustrator: **Laura Middleton**
Food Stylist: **Rachel de Thample**
Nutritional advice: **Ciara Jean Roberts**
Production: **Nic Jones and Gemma John**

A Cataloguing in Publication record for this
title is available from the British Library.

Colour reproduction by f1 colour, London.
Printed and bound in China by C&C Offset
Printing Co., Ltd.

Important note: The information and advice contained in this book are intended as a
general guide and are not specific to individuals or their particular circumstances. Many
plant substances, whether sold as foods or as medicines and used externally or internally,
can cause an allergic reaction in some people. Neither the author nor the publishers can
be held responsible for claims arising from the inappropriate use of any remedy. Do
not attempt self-diagnosis or self-treatment for serious or long-term conditions before
consulting a medical professional or qualified practitioner. Do not undertake any self-
treatment while taking other prescribed drugs or receiving therapy without first seeking
professional guidance. Always seek medical advice if any symptoms persist.

Contents

Introduction

People around the world have been brewing tonics, teas and tisanes for thousands of years as a way of keeping themselves healthy, energised and nutritionally balanced. Many of these ancient remedies are as delicious as they are good for you, and for some time now I have incorporated them into my daily routine, under the guidance of nutritional therapist, and friend, Ciara Jean Roberts. As you will find if you do likewise, they will not only quench your thirst but also offer a whole range of nourishing and healing properties.

Simply starting your day with some turmeric in a Golden Chai (page 77) can reduce arthritic symptoms – I was getting achy joints, so swapped it for my morning coffee and it truly made a difference. My mother had high blood pressure, which drinking Beetroot Kvass (page 27) almost instantly reduced.

Whenever possible, choose organic ingredients, as they are free of pesticides and grown in soil that is rich with nutrients and minerals. Non-organic soil is full of chemical inputs, meaning they are not only on your food, but in it, too. Secondly, filter your water or opt for bottled mineral water that comes from a natural spring. Most tap water is treated with chlorine which counteracts many of the benefits and can kill off any fermented foods. Lastly, don't be tempted to use honey instead of sugar in the fermented recipes; the antibacterial qualities of honey will kill off your cultures. This is particularly important with kefir and kombucha. Opt, instead, for organic raw, unrefined sugar. Or experiment with Palmyra jaggery, which is a traditional Ayurvedic ingredient that offers more nutritional value.

I've aimed to include a mix of drinks to give you a true taste of a variety of cultures. Hopefully, you'll find lots of opportunities to weave them into your day and to call upon them in times of need – whenever insomnia strikes, anxiety hits or you just want a delicious non-alcoholic brew.

Here's to drinking to your health!

Using tonics and teas safely

The more one-to-one work I do with people, the more I come to understand that each person is unique and what works for one might not be so great for another. Plants contain powerful components that can work wonders for the human body. It is important, however, to realise that they need to be used with great respect. They contain chemicals that send signals to our cells, so they really do have an effect.

As you peruse the beautiful recipes that Rachel has put together, ask yourself, 'What calls to me?' 'What is my medicine for today?' Choose your tonic or a tea according to your mood and also consider the time of year. What is most seasonally appropriate? It might be that a simple mug of lemon in hot water is just the ticket, or you might need something more therapeutic. The body is always changing, as is our mood, so see what sings to your cells on any given day.

The introduction of the right tonic or tea at the optimum time can make a life-changing difference. I had a client a few years ago who was in his early thirties and about to go onto heavy medication (methotrexate) for rheumatoid arthritis, which might have impacted his fertility when he and his wife were looking to conceive a second child. I prescribed turmeric tea – simply a teaspoon of powder in warm water daily with breakfast – and this reduced his symptoms within just a few weeks. No meds were required and he went on to have a beautiful baby girl.

It is important, however, to be mindful of what may or may not be appropriate for you. Many herbs should be avoided if you are pregnant or lactating, for example, while if you have any blood-sugar issues – if you are pre-diabetic or diabetic, for example – you should avoid recipes containing sugar. If you are taking medication, check for contraindications, and take particular care if you suffer from impaired kidney or liver function. If it feels wrong, don't do it. Learn to really tune into your own body and its signals and how to best nourish yourself. Consider the therapeutic window of some of these offerings; administer a cough tonic as soon as you feel the onset of symptoms, for example. If you are taking a tea or tonic to help with a particular minor health complaint, do seek medical advice from a professional if the symptoms do not improve within a few days.

Fermented food and drink is a growing trend and there can be many benefits to including these, but if you are not accustomed to them, go easy and start with very small amounts. They will influence the gut flora, which, if it has been out of balance, can take a bit of time to recalibrate.

Let these recipes inspire you, and be playful with them. The energy and intention you put into making them also has an effect on how they will resonate in your body. The ritual of making a tea or a tonic for yourself or for loved ones is all part of the process. I see much improvement in people struggling with sleep when they introduce a bedtime tea, and I believe that this is due not only to the combination of ingredients in the tea but also to the fact that they are taking time to create something beneficial for themselves. The greater the amount of joy you can stir into your potion, the better!

Ciara Jean Roberts
Naturopathic Nutritional Therapist and Yoga Teacher

Tonics

Seasonal ginger shots

Ginger truly does top the list of effective natural home remedies. Used throughout history by different cultures around the world, ginger harnesses incredible healing power: not only does it help settle upset tummies and soothe migraines, but numerous studies suggest it can protect against cancer. Opt for organic, where possible.

Below are my favourite ginger shot combinations. Peel and juice the ginger first, then feed the herb or spice through the juicer. Finally, juice the fruit. Each of the following makes 1 shot.

Asian pear drop

2cm piece of ginger, ¼ stick of lemongrass and ½ pear

Persian ginger

2cm piece of ginger, 1 tablespoon fresh (non-sprayed) rose petals or ¼ teaspoon rose water and 15 pitted cherries

Sunshine ginger

2cm piece of ginger, 1 blood orange or 2 clementines and a dusting of cinnamon

Solo ginger

2cm piece of ginger, ¼ lemon (zest and all) and a dusting of cayenne pepper

Blushing ginger

2cm piece of ginger, 2 cardamom pods (feed it whole through your juicer or grind the seeds and add after juicing), 4cm piece of rhubarb and 1 small or ½ medium-sized beetroot

Winter ginger

2cm slice of ginger, 1 apple and a drop of oregano essential oil

Lime and cayenne pepper shot

Doctors used to carry little jars of cayenne pepper in case of cardiac emergencies, as it has a powerful effect on circulation and blood pressure. Start with a small amount of cayenne pepper the first time, then slowly increase it.

Makes 1 shot

¼ teaspoon cayenne pepper

Juice of ½ lime

50ml water

½ teaspoon raw honey or maple syrup

Whisk the cayenne with the lime juice, top it up with water and sweeten to taste with honey or maple syrup.

Knock it back first thing in the morning, followed by a glass of cold water, and feel your energy levels rise.

Charcoal shot

Activated charcoal is like a magnet for toxins and is used in emergency medicine in cases of accidental poisoning. It's great to clear your system. Take at night and drink a large glass of water upon waking, followed by sufficient amounts of water during the day to assist the elimination process.

Makes 1 shot

1 activated charcoal tablet

50ml freshly made apple or pineapple juice (or water)

A squeeze of lime

½ teaspoon aloe vera (see page 21), or use bottled aloe

Whisk everything together and drink straight away.

Turmeric shots

If you need a mid-morning or afternoon energy boost,
opt for one of these shots rather than a hit of espresso.
It'll give you the sustained lift you need, whilst also
delivering turmeric's numerous other health benefits.

Turmeric, pineapple and black pepper shot
Juice 1 thumb-sized piece each of peeled turmeric and pineapple and
add a pinch of finely ground pepper.

Turmeric, carrot and cayenne shot
Juice 1 thumb-sized piece of peeled turmeric with 1 carrot. Finish with
a squeeze of lemon or lime and a pinch of cayenne.

Turmeric, almond milk and cardamom shot
This is more like a smoothie shot. Blend 1 thumb-sized piece of peeled
turmeric with 100ml almond or coconut milk and the ground seeds of
1 cardamom pod.

Lemon, lavender and peppermint shot

Essential oils are concentrated plant power, and they can be hugely effective when applied in the right way for you and your unique constitution. Note that it is important you use food-grade essential oils as other grades are not safe to ingest. The combination of lemon, lavender and peppermint is immensely refreshing. I use it to clear sinus blockages, which I typically get after travelling. This is also a very soothing shot to take if you have a migraine. Admittedly, it tastes rather unusual, but the effects, which are almost instant, make it worthwhile.

Makes 1 shot

2 drops lemon essential oil (food grade)

2 drops peppermint essential oil (food grade)

2 drops lavender essential oil (food grade)

100ml filtered or mineral water

Add the essential oil drops to a glass and top up with water. Mix well, knock it back and follow it with a fresh glass of water.

Repeat up to three times a day until symptoms subside. As always, if symptoms do not improve after a few days, seek medical advice.

Everyday health tonic

This tonic is a brilliant booster for everyday health and a must-have remedy to use during flu season. The ginger helps to calm inflammation and create internal heat. The cayenne acts to boost circulation and horseradish is a decongestant, while garlic and onion help with overall immunity. Opt for fresh, organic ingredients to maximise benefits, and if one of the them is unavailable, simply double up on one of the other ingredients if you like.

Makes 6 x 50ml shots

2 tablespoons chopped garlic

2 tablespoons chopped onion

2 tablespoons grated fresh ginger

2 tablespoons grated horseradish root

2 tablespoons chopped cayenne peppers (or any seasonally available hot peppers)

350ml raw apple cider vinegar

Pile the garlic, onion, ginger, horseradish and peppers into a 350ml lidded jar. Fill the jar with raw apple cider vinegar. Close the lid tightly and shake. Store in a cool dark place.

Shake at least once a day for two weeks. Then, filter the tonic through a clean piece of muslin, pour into a sterilised bottle and label. It will keep at room temperature for up to 6 months.

Take as soon as you feel the symptoms of a cold in 50ml shots three times daily, before food. Avoid taking vinegar internally if you have a stomach ulcer.

HOW TO STERILISE JARS
Wash jars and bottles in very hot, soapy water. Dry with a clean cloth then place in an oven, without the lids, at 100°C/Gas ¼ for 10 minutes. Bottling and sealing drinks while the liquid and container are still hot increases shelf life and decreases risk of spoilage.

Garlic and lemon elixir

This is an easy-to-make, all-round cleansing elixir. Garlic and lemon are a powerful anti-bacterial partnership. In clinical studies, garlic has been shown to significantly lower cholesterol and in Germany, it is sometimes used for the treatment of atherosclerosis (hardening or blocking of arteries). It has also long been used for the prevention of infections, colds and flu. The whole lemon supports the immune system by having an alkalising effect, while limonene, a compound found in the peel of citrus fruits, helps reduce inflammation.

Makes 20 x 50ml shots

2 lemons

2 heads of garlic (or 20 cloves)

1 litre filtered or mineral water

Blitz the lemon and garlic (peel, pith and all) in a food-processor or blender.

Transfer to a small saucepan, add the water and simmer for 15 minutes. Bring the mixture very slowly up to boiling point then turn off the heat immediately. Let the mixture cool down naturally.

Once at room temperature, strain the liquid, pour into sterilised bottles and discard the pulp. Store the elixir in the fridge, it will keep for 3 weeks.

Drink one 50ml shot per day, 2 hours before or after your main meal. Continue this for 3 weeks. Take a break for 1 week, then make a new mix and repeat for a further 3 weeks.

After about 3 weeks, you will feel a youthful regeneration of your whole body.

Cough tonic

There are many potent ingredients here that create a powerful rejuvenating and soothing tonic to alleviate coughs. Use raw, cold-pressed honey as opposed to commercially heated honey to get the full nutritional and anti-bacterial benefits from it. The citrus juice adds vitamin C to aid a swifter recovery, while both ginger and turmeric have powerful anti-inflammatory properties.

Makes 4 x 125ml servings

30g fresh oregano and/or thyme

2cm piece of fresh ginger, peeled and grated

2cm piece of fresh turmeric, peeled and grated

5 whole black peppercorns

2 garlic cloves, grated

500ml filtered or mineral water

2 tablespoons raw honey or maple syrup

2 tablespoons fresh lime or lemon juice

Blend the oregano, ginger, turmeric, peppercorns, garlic, and water in a blender or food-processor (or roughly crush the dry ingredients in a pestle and mortar and then add the water). Pour into a medium saucepan and simmer for 15 minutes.

Whisk in the honey or maple syrup and citrus juice to combine. Strain though a piece of muslin, pushing on the herbs to squeeze out as much liquid as possible, then pour into a sterilised bottle.

Drink a 125ml mug of warmed cough tonic once or twice a day until your cough subsides. Sip slowly to allow the body to gently assimilate it.

Nettle tonic

Nettles are one of the most nutrient-dense wild foods that are readily available to us. They have a good reputation as an iron tonic, not just because they contain relatively high levels of iron but also because they contain amino acids and vitamin C, which are both required for iron absorption. If you are vegetarian or vegan, nettles are one of the best things you can include in your diet to ensure your blood stays healthy. Nettles cause a stinging reaction when you touch them, so use gardening gloves when gathering them. Cooking removes their sting.

Serves 2

2 handfuls of nettles

4 apples, roughly chopped

½ lemon roughly chopped (peel and all)

6 sprigs fresh mint

Place the nettles in a sieve and rinse well. Pour boiling water over the nettles to deactivate their sting. Feed everything through your juicer. Drink straight away.

Aloe cooler

Aloe vera is believed to be deeply soothing to the intestinal tissue, which makes this shot a great choice for digestive complaints. It also said to have a cooling effect and that it can help mend internal scar tissue (it's widely used topically for burns). Drink this once or twice a day – or simply have 1–2 tablespoons of aloe juice on its own – as a remedy or just for delicious refreshment. When sourcing aloe, ensure the variety is bred for internal consumption or use a pure juice. You can buy large aloe leaves from organic green grocers or health food shops.

Makes 1 x 150ml serving

4cm piece of fresh, edible aloe (e.g. Aloe barbadensis) or 2 tablespoons aloe juice

150ml coconut water

A squeeze of lime

Wash the aloe and place it on a plate flat side up. Using a sharp knife, slice off the top rind. Cut into 4cm cubes. Rinse off the sticky latex coating the clear flesh (it's the flesh you want, not the gooey latex, which can be an irritant). Freeze what you don't want to use straight away.

Blend this with the coconut water and add a squeeze of lime.

Green juices

Wheatgrass and gooseberry

Wheatgrass juice is an effective healer because it contains
a wealth of minerals and vitamins. It is also extremely rich
in protein, can improve blood sugar, detoxify the liver and
so much more. Some even claim that it can help keep your
hair from greying! When gooseberries are out of season,
swap with 4 apples and a squeeze of lime juice.

Serves 2

3–4 handfuls of wheatgrass

250g gooseberries

Feed everything through your juicer. Drink straight away.

Chlorella and coconut water

Gram for gram, chlorella, a Japanese alga, is
more nutrient dense than broccoli and kale.
It also contains high amounts of protein.
Coconut water is very nourishing to the
kidneys, so helps prevent dehydration.

Serves 2

1 tablespoon
chlorella powder

350ml coconut water

Simply whisk the chlorella powder
into the coconut water and drink.
Alternatively, add the powder to a
bottle of coconut water then shake
and drink on the go.

Apple and parsley juice

Fresh parsley contains high levels of both
iron and vitamin C, making it a good herb to
include for blood health, especially if you are
experiencing iron deficiency (anaemia).

Serves 2

4 apples

30g parsley

½ lemon

Roughly chop all the ingredients and feed them through
your juicer. Include all the bits of the lemon (zest, pith and
flesh) for maximum benefits.

Celery and coriander juice

Celery can help to regulate levels of hydrochloric
acid in the stomach. Coriander is a very useful
herb in heavy-metal detoxification and also helps
kill off intestinal parasites.

Serves 2

6 celery sticks

2 pears

30g coriander

½ lime,
including peel

Roughly chop all the ingredients and feed them through
your juicer. Drink straight away.

Jamu kunyit

The Balinese equivalent to 'an apple a day', this ancient turmeric tonic, which families in Bali have been brewing up for more than 5,000 years, is said to keep your health problems at bay. They also call it the 'love potion' as it's believed to have an aphrodisiac effect. Try it and see...

Makes 4 x 125ml servings

4 thumb-sized pieces of fresh turmeric, peeled and grated

A thumb-sized piece of fresh ginger, peeled and grated

1 tablespoon tamarind paste or the pulp from 2 whole tamarind

500ml filtered or mineral water

2–3 tablespoons raw honey, maple syrup or coconut palm sugar

A pinch of ground pepper (black or cubeb)

Blend the turmeric, ginger and tamarind with the water either in a food-processor or with a stick blender. Alternatively, pound everything to a paste and let it infuse for 30 minutes.

Strain though muslin into a sterilised jar. Sweeten to taste with honey, maple syrup or coconut palm sugar and stir in a pinch of pepper. Drink straight away or chill. It will keep in the fridge for up to 1 week.

Beetroot kvass

A beautiful, blushing, probiotic drink made with whey – a product that typically gets wasted but is loaded with nutrients and is a useful source of amino acids. At times when your appetite is low due to illness, whey can be a useful way to keep protein intake up. Beetroot provides a wonderful boost of nitric oxide, which has a positive effect on the vascular system and arterial velocity. Keep the peel on the beetroot as it contains bacteria that helps kickstart fermentation. Just ensure you thoroughly wash them first.

Makes 750ml

2 medium-sized beetroot, peel left on and cut into 2–3cm pieces

1 teaspoon sea salt or Himalayan pink salt

4 tablespoons fresh whey or buttermilk*

700ml of filtered or mineral water

Whey is a by-product of making cheese or labneh (strained yogurt), but buttermilk works just as well

Put the beetroot into a 1-litre jar. Sprinkle over the salt and add the whey or buttermilk.

Pour in the water, ensuring you leave a 5cm gap at the top of the jar, and stir well. Loosely fit a lid and leave in a cool, dark place for 2–5 days.

When the kvass is effervescent, transfer to the refrigerator. It will keep for 2 months.

Medicinal vinegars

Apple cider vinegar is one of the best kitchen remedies. It can help lower blood glucose, blood pressure and bad cholesterol. Take 1–2 tablespoons daily (not more, as too much can be counterproductive). Opt for organic, raw cider vinegar, preferably with the mother culture.

Fill a sterilised jar about one-third with your chosen herb, then pour in apple cider vinegar until the jar is full. Cover tightly and leave for 14 days in a cool, dark place, shaking well daily. Strain and pour into a sterilised bottle. Store in a dark, cool place for up to 1 year.

Rosemary	Useful for low energy and poor circulation, digestion, nerves and for increasing focus and concentration. Avoid daily use if you're pregnant.
Sage	Antifungal, antibacterial and antiviral. Avoid using over an extended period of time or if you are pregnant or breastfeeding.
Thyme	Antiviral and antibacterial. Useful for upper respiratory infections, coughs and bronchitis.
Oregano	Antiviral and antibacterial. Useful for upper respiratory infections.
Bee balm (Monarda)	Antibacterial, helpful for thick congested coughs, sore throat and fever.
Mint	Stomach-soothing digestive aid. Avoid if you have problems with the pyloric sphincter.
Rose petals	Astringent and anti-inflammatory. Medicine for the heart.
Elderflowers	Boost the immune system. Useful for sore throats.
Blackcurrant leaves	Packed with vitamin C, just like the fruit. Also rich in antioxidants that have powerful anti-inflammatory properties.

Cherry Vanilla Shrub

I make all kinds of shrubs, also known as 'drinking vinegars', both as a refreshing healthy drink and to capture seasonal moments, especially in the summer, when juicy, sun-kissed fruits are in abundance. The best and easiest way to make these is without following a recipe. Just pile your fruit into a sterilised jar, cover with vinegar and sweeten to taste with honey or maple syrup. You can add spices or herbs, too, if you like. This version uses the classic combination of cherries and vanilla. To drink, simply strain the fruit out (you can eat it – try it in salads) and pour into a tumbler with ice. Top up with sparkling or a good-quality tonic water. You can also add a shrub shot to a smoothie or use it to make virgin cocktails.

Makes 500ml

300g fresh cherries, pitted

500ml raw cider vinegar

2–3 tablespoons raw honey or maple syrup

½ vanilla pod

Put the pitted cherries into a sealed bottle, top up with the cider vinegar and sweeten with honey or maple syrup to taste. Add the vanilla. Secure the lid and let it mature at room temperature for at least 1 week, or for up to 6 months in the fridge – the vinegar will preserve the fruit.

Strain into glasses over ice and top up with sparkling mineral water – you want roughly 1 part shrub to 2 parts water. Spoon a few cherries into the glasses, too, or use them in salads or other dishes such as tagines.

Elderberry syrup with echinacea

Both elderberries and echinacea are powerful immune system boosters and have been used to prevent and treat colds and flus for many years. Ginger is also added for its antimicrobial, antibiotic and anti-inflammatory properties. Mix all of these immune powerhouses together to give your nasty cold or flu a good beating!

Makes 500ml

50g dried or 100g fresh elderberries

500ml filtered or mineral water

¼ cup dried echinacea root or 1 teaspoon echinacea tincture

3cm piece of fresh ginger, peeled and thinly sliced

1 cinnamon stick

6 cloves

Zest and juice of 1 orange

125g raw honey

Put the elderberries and water into a saucepan along with the echinacea (if using the root), ginger, cinnamon, cloves and orange zest and juice. Bring to a rolling boil then turn down the heat and simmer for 30 minutes, or until it is the consistency of maple syrup. It should be thick enough to coat the back of a spoon.

Leave to cool, then strain everything through a fine sieve lined with a muslin cloth (one you don't mind being stained purple!). Whisk in the honey and the echinacea (if using tincture).

Pour into sterilised bottles and store in the fridge for up to 3 months.

If you start to feel a cold or flu coming on – or even if you're just around people who are sick – take a few tablespoons of this throughout the day. If you do get sick, you can take a spoonful every couple of hours. Avoid taking it for more than a week or two at a time, however, as you also need to give your body a break from the herbs and maximise the therapeutic window.

Rosehip syrup

Rosehip syrup is dripping with vitamin C and has long had a reputation for keeping colds at bay. It has a surprisingly tropical tang, with notes of lychee and mango. Diluted with about five parts of cold water, it makes a delicious cordial drink, which kids will love.

Makes 250ml

250g fresh rosehips

350ml filtered or mineral water

125g raw honey or maple syrup

Roughly chop the rosehips in a food-processor then transfer to a saucepan and add the water. Bring to the boil, then turn the heat down and simmer for about 15 minutes.

Strain through a double layer of muslin, letting the pulp sit for at least 30 minutes so that all the juice passes through. Press with a wooden spoon to squeeze out as much of the remaining liquid as possible.

Gently heat the extracted juice until just warmed through. Remove from the heat and whisk in the honey or maple syrup.

Pour the syrup into a sterilised bottle or jar while it's still hot. Seal and use within 3 months. Refrigerate once opened. Take 1–2 tablespoons daily to help keep colds at bay.

Dandelion and burdock cordial

Dandelion is a useful liver tonic as it helps to increase the flow of bile, which is important in the digestive process for the breakdown of fat and the removal of waste products. Burdock is a blood purifier and lymph cleanser. It also contains the fibre inulin that helps to bulk the stool as it has a significant capacity to absorb water, hence promoting smoother stool transit. Wood avens is a beautiful plant whose roots impart a cinnamon-like flavour. You can use fresh or dried roots for this recipe or, if unavailable, substitute it with a cinnamon stick. You can dig up fresh roots from your garden – just be sure you know what you're looking for. If not, you can order dried roots online (see page 92 for suppliers).

Makes 400ml

15g wood avens roots (or 1 cinnamon stick)

50g dandelion roots

50g burdock roots

1 thumb-sized piece of ginger, peeled and chopped

12 cloves

750ml filtered or mineral water

100g maple syrup

If using fresh roots, clean them thoroughly before roughly chopping.

Place all the ingredients except the maple syrup in a pan and boil for 15 minutes.

Strain into a clean jug. Whisk in the maple syrup.

The cordial will keep in the fridge for a couple of weeks. Serve diluted with chilled soda water.

Brain booster

Brahmi, used in this tonic, is named after the Hindu God Brahman, believed by Hindus to be the all-pervading consciousness responsible for all 'creative forces' in the world. Brahmi is traditionally known as a nervine tonic, soothing anxiety and tension and calming the mind and body, promoting relaxation. It is beneficial for promoting mental clarity, alertness and short- and long-term memory, while relieving mental fatigue. It is mild and gentle, so safe for children and adults alike.

Makes 2 x 250ml servings

75g walnuts

3 pitted dates

1 teaspoon vanilla extract or seeds from ½ vanilla pod

½ teaspoon ground cinnamon

2 teaspoons brahmi mushroom extract

500ml filtered or mineral water

Whiz everything together in a blender or food-processor, slowly adding the water until well mixed. Strain through a fine mesh sieve for a smoother consistency.

Drink immediately or chill until ready to drink. It will keep in the fridge for 2 days.

Milk kefir

Kefir originated in parts of Eastern Europe and Southwest Asia. The name is derived from the Turkish word keyif, which means 'feeling good' after eating. Kefir contains about 30 different micro-organisms, making it a much more potent source of probiotics than other fermented dairy products. The nutritional content of kefir will vary depending on the milk quality and length of fermentation. It is high in B12, an important nutrient for the nervous system.

Makes 600ml

600ml full-fat cow's milk, or coconut or almond milk*

1 tablespoon milk kefir grains

1 dried fig, quartered (optional)

A dusting of cinnamon, to serve (optional)

* Opt for organic cow's milk – even better if it's unhomogenised or raw. If using almond milk, blend with two dates and strain before using – the grains need sugars to feed them, which other milks have naturally.

Mix the milk and kefir grains in a sterilised 1-litre jar. Add the dried fig, too, if using – it will help speed up the fermentation process and also adds a lovely flavour.

Cover the jar with a cloth and leave in a warm place for 12–24 hours. The mixture will thicken, become slightly tangy and a little fizzy. Strain and store in the fridge until ready to consume.

The kefir will keep for some time but will continue to ferment in the fridge. It's best consumed within 2 weeks.

STORING MILK KEFIR GRAINS
To keep the kefir grains for your next batch, store them in a jar, covered with any type of milk, and place in the fridge.

Water kefir

Water kefir has been consumed for hundreds of years. In the late 1800s, the grains were used in Mexico to ferment a drink made from the sweetened juice of the prickly pear cactus. Other documentation traces their use to Tibet, the Caucasus Mountains, and the southern peninsula of Ukraine. The benefits are similar to dairy-based kefir – the grains contain more than 30 strains of beneficial bacteria – so this is a brilliant drink if you can't consume dairy products.

Makes 4 x 250ml servings

3 tablespoons unrefined caster sugar

1 litre filtered or mineral water or coconut water

2 tablespoons water kefir grains

2 tablespoons dried fruit such as mango, sour cherries, or fig (optional)

2 slices of lemon, lime or orange (optional)

Whisk the sugar and water together until the sugar dissolves. Pour into a sterilised 1.5-litre jar. Add the kefir grains and the dried fruit and citrus slices, if using.

Cover with a clean cloth or double layer of muslin. Set in a dark, cool place to ferment for 2 days. The kefir should have a mild apple cider vinegar tang to it and have the fizz of sparkling water.

Strain the kefir grains through a plastic sieve or a colander lined with a muslin cloth (avoid metal as it can de-active the grains). Pour the kefir into sterilised bottles and chill until ready to drink. It will keep in the fridge for up to 3 weeks.

REUSING KEFIR GRAINS
Keep using the kefir grains or store them in enough brewed water kefir from your last batch, in the fridge, for up to 2 weeks between batches. They need to be fed as least every fortnight to keep their potency.

Tropical detox smoothie

Papaya seeds, pumpkin seeds and cloves are all hugely effective in getting rid of intestinal parasites and are great, all-round digestive cleansers. Pineapple has many benefits due to its powerful enzyme ingredient, bromelain, which acts as a marvellous digestive enzyme to help break down food and aid nutrient assimilation. It is also helpful for those with allergies and sinusitis. The highest bromelain content is found in the core, so be sure to use that part too. This recipe would serve as a wonderful tonic to aid recovery from surgery and injury.

Serves 2

½ papaya (including the seeds)

¼ pineapple, peeled

4 freshly ground cloves

2 tablespoons coconut oil

2 tablespoons desiccated coconut

2 tablespoons pumpkin seeds (soaked overnight if possible)

500ml coconut water

Blend the fruit (flesh and seeds) with the cloves, coconut oil, desiccated coconut, pumpkin seeds (drain first if you soaked overnight) and coconut water until as smooth as possible – it will be quite textured. Add a little more coconut water to thin if necessary. Drink straight away.

Teas

Loose leaf teas

The world of tea is vast and can easily be likened to the world of wine. Like wine, there are many different terroirs that lend to a tea's unique profile. When tea is picked, which part of the plant is harvested and how it is processed thereafter also plays a part in determining the flavour. And that's focusing on camellia sinensis, just one species of evergreen shrub or small tree whose leaves and buds are used to produce tea.

Looking at tisanes made from herbs, spices and flowers opens up a whole other world of flavours to tantalise the taste buds, and strengthen body and mind. There is a wonderful array of herbal, Ayurvedic and alternative teas available in shops these days. Buying a few basics (see page 92) and brewing up your own blends is often cheaper, fresher, more flavourful and fun than buying them – and they make wonderful gifts, too.

How to make your own tea bags

Buy unbleached muslin – either a whole roll or individual pieces – and cut into small squares of approximately 7cm. Place roughly 1 tablespoon of loose-leaf tea (more or less, depending on the blend) in the centre of each square and pull the corners up together, ensuring there is enough space for the tea leaves to move around. Secure with string.

If you want to compost the tea bags, ensure the fabric and string are fully compostable. Alternatively, buy ready-to-fill tea bags online. Ensure you opt for non-bleached varieties, as bleach is not good for you and would cancel out the benefits of a beautiful homemade tea or tisane blend.

Jasmine tea   Regarded in Chinese medicine as a herb with balanced character, jasmine flowers – used to scent tea – can relieve the blood vessels around your eyes and help relax muscles, making it a lovely tea to enjoy after a long day. Brew 2 tablespoons of leaves with 3 tablespoons cold water, topped up with 250ml freshly boiled water. The mix of cold and hot water makes a more full bodied tea. Steep for 3 minutes. Re-infuse two or three times.

White tea   White teas are the least processed of all teas – with fresh spring flower, melon, cucumber and honey flavours – and are reputed for helping maintain healthy, youthful skin. Silver Needle (pictured), the most famous white tea, is composed only of young leaf buds. Brew 2 tablespoons of leaves with 3 tablespoons cold water, topped up with 250ml freshly boiled water. Steep for 3 minutes. Re-infuse two or three times.

Green tea   From China's expertly fired Dragon Well and the exuberant flavours of Anji Green, to the delicately vegetal character of the steamed or shaded green teas of Japan, such as Gyokuro (pictured), green teas cover a broad spectrum of flavours. Leaves are picked at the beginning of spring and are energy-dense with a bundle of health benefits: reputed to lower the risk of cancer and reduce cholesterol, for example. Brew 1 heaped tablespoon with 2–3 tablespoons cold water topped up with 200ml freshly boiled water. Steep for 3 minutes. Re-infuse two or three times.

Oolong tea   Complex flavours in oolong teas derive from repeated stages of oxidisation, shaping and firing. They're often highly aromatic, with floral and biscuity flavours. They are a great antioxidant and can protect against tooth decay. Brew 1 heaped tablespoon with 250ml freshly boiled water. Steep for 5 minutes. Re-infuse two or three times.

Puerh tea   Puerh teas are highly revered in China, where the processing methods have remained a well-guarded secret for centuries. The tea is fermented before being aged and packed into bricks. The careful ageing process adds a fascinating dimension to the flavour, maturing the tea into something richer, smoother, mellower and more complex, without losing the original life of the young fresh leaf. Puerh is brilliant for settling the digestive system after a heavy meal and is also said to aid in weight loss. Brew 1 heaped teaspoon or 1 mini puerh cake with 150ml freshly boiled water. Steep for 7 minutes. Re-infuse two or three times.

Olive leaf tea   Olive leaves have been consumed throughout history, in powdered form, tinctures and as a tea. They contain compounds with antioxidant and anti-inflammatory properties. Basically, their nutritional value is similar to that of a good quality olive oil. You can dry olive tree leaves to make your own tea. Brew 1 tablespoon for 10 minutes with 250ml freshly boiled water.

Detox teas

Lemon verbena and calendula tea

Lemon verbena and calendula are soothing to the gut. Calendula contains high amounts of flavonoids that help relax muscles and increase blood flow, which aids menstrual cramps. The lemon verbena provides a soothing partner and has been shown to increase white blood cells, so is a boost for the immune system.

Makes 1 x 250ml serving

2 tablespoons fresh or dried lemon verbena

1 teaspoon dried or 1 tablespoon fresh calendula petals

300ml freshly boiled water

Add the lemon verbena and calendula to a teapot and pour over the freshly boiled water. Steep for 10 minutes then strain into a mug. Drink warm, or chill and drink cold.

Spiced dandelion tea

This rich, earthy brew is more like a light coffee and is packed with ingredients to make you glow. Dandelion roots have a diuretic action that helps cleanse the body without depleting it. Star anise helps clear the digestive system as does cardamom, which also reduces toxins in the blood and skin. Liquorice can help manage negative effects of excessive adrenaline and is anti-inflammatory, helping the skin inside and out.

Makes 1 x 250ml serving

1 tablespoon dried dandelion root

1 star anise

3 cardamom pods

½ dried liquorice root or 1 teaspoon dried, shredded liquorice

300ml freshly boiled water

Place all the ingredients in a teapot and pour over the freshly boiled water. Steep for 15 minutes then strain into a mug.

Elderflower and lemon tea

The distinctive lacy blooms of the elderflower have been used medicinally for more than four thousand years in different cultures due to their anti-inflammatory and antiseptic properties. Elderflower is rich in flavonoids, including quercetin, hence its ability to calm systemic inflammation. The vibrant combination of elderflower with fresh lemon is one to lift the spirits.

Makes 1 x 300ml serving

A slice of lemon

1 tablespoons dried elderflower*

200ml freshly boiled water

Use 2 tablespoons of fresh elderflowers when they are in season. You can dry fresh flowers, too, so you can enjoy this tea all year-round.

Bundle the lemon slice and elderflower into a teapot. Cover with the freshly boiled water and top up with 100ml cold water. Steep for 5 minutes then strain into a mug.

Chicory chai

The inulin in chicory root is also known as a prebiotic fibre because it's highly fermentable when it reacts with the friendly bacteria in the gut. Prebiotics can help promote the growth of helpful probiotics in your digestive system and may enhance calcium absorption. This is why you're likely to see inulin, or chicory root fibre, in probiotic supplements. The classic mix of chai spices give it an added boost as these warming ingredients are great for digestive health.

Makes 1 x 275ml serving

2 tablespoons chicory coffee powder

½ cinnamon stick or ¼ teaspoon ground cinnamon

6 cloves

4 black peppercorns

A grating of nutmeg

1cm slice of fresh ginger, peeled

3 crushed cardamom pods

300ml coconut, almond or hazelnut milk

A drop of raw honey or maple syrup (optional)

Place all the ingredients in a saucepan and simmer for 15–20 minutes. Strain out the spices and serve warm.

If you want a faster infusion, use a coffee grinder to grind all the spices to a powder. Add to the milk and chicory powder in a saucepan and simmer for just 5 minutes. Strain and serve. Sweeten with a hint of honey or maple syrup, if you like.

VARIATIONS
CHOCOLATE CHAI: Replace the chicory powder with raw cacao powder.
ROOIBOS CHAI: Replace the chicory powder with loose rooibos tea leaves or two rooibos tea bags.
CHAI COFFEE: Replace the chicory powder with 200ml freshly brewed coffee and halve the quantity of milk.

Citrus wake-up calls

As simple as it seems, starting your day with a mug of hot water with lemon really does make a difference to your health. A fabulous way to hydrate after the long hours of sleep, it also helps to freshen up the whole system. Lemon will gently stimulate the liver, and drinking with warm water is better as it doesn't require the body to expend energy warming up cold fluids. If you want a little twist to your morning citrus routine, try one of the following brews, which have additional health benefits.

Morning sunshine

Makes 1 x 250ml serving

2 clementines

3cm piece fresh ginger, peeled and thinly sliced

1 small turmeric root, peeled and thinly sliced

250ml freshly boiled water

Clementines and ginger contain lots of vitamin C, which is good for skin. There's plenty of orange colour here, indicating the presence of carotenes, which are good for eye health. Ginger and turmeric together create a strong anti-inflammatory action.

Halve the clementines and squeeze the juice into a teapot. Add the squeezed fruit, along with the ginger and turmeric. Pour over the freshly boiled water to cover. Steep for 5 minutes or longer then strain into a mug.

Sicilian garden tea

Makes 1 x 250ml serving

1 lemon

2 rosemary sprigs

1 cinnamon stick

250ml freshly boiled water

Aromatic rosemary has an uplifting and invigorating effect and the cinnamon helps to balance blood sugar levels. This tea makes for a great start to the day and is a lovely twist on classic lemon tea.

Strip the lemon zest using a vegetable peeler and put into a teapot, then squeeze the juice into the teapot. Add the rosemary and cinnamon and pour over the freshly boiled water. Steep for 5 minutes then strain into a mug.

Cosy bedtime tea

The ritual of making a bedtime tea can be enough to calm the mind. Chamomile and lavender sooth the nervous system and tone the parasympathetic nervous system, stimulating our 'rest-and-digest' mode – the ideal state before bed. Chamomile also helps to reduce excess cortisol, a stress hormone which can be damaging in large amounts. Chamomile can ease stomach cramps and may also be helpful in preventing migraines. Take twice a day to ease menstrual cramping. Use with caution or avoid altogether if you are pregnant or attempting to conceive.

Makes 1 x 250ml serving

2 teaspoons chamomile

1 teaspoon lavender

A grating of nutmeg

250ml freshly boiled water

Combine the chamomile, lavender and nutmeg in a teapot and pour over the freshly boiled water. Steep 5 minutes then strain into a mug.

Sweet dreams

This combination is a beautiful tea for the nervous system. Lemon balm is also useful for soothing an upset stomach. Be mindful if you are hypothyroid as lemon balm can inhibit thyroid function so take only in small amounts. This is not an issue in healthy thyroid function.

Makes 1 x 250ml serving

1 tablespoon fresh or dried lemon balm leaves

2 teaspoon dried lime flowers or 2 tablespoons fresh lime flowers

1 teaspoon dried rose buds or 1 tablespoon fresh rose petals

250ml freshly boiled water

Put the lemon balm, lime flowers and rose buds or petals into a teapot and pour over the freshly boiled water. Top up with 50ml cold water. Steep for 10 minutes then strain into a mug. Drink warm.

Grasshopper tea

The amino acid L-theanine in green tea helps to promote a calm alertness, while the mint adds an uplifting aroma and also helps to freshen the breath. A great drink when you're in need of some clarity and focus, this tea can be taken regularly – so embrace your inner grasshopper!

Makes 1 x 300ml serving

2 teaspoons green tea leaves or 1 green tea bag

A large handful of fresh mint or 1 peppermint tea bag

200ml freshly boiled water

Place the green tea and fresh mint or mint tea bag in a teapot. Pour over the freshly boiled water and top up with 100ml cold water. Steep for 5 minutes then strain into a mug. Drink warm.

Nettle and mint tea

Nettles are a great kidney cleanser and can reduce kidney inflammation (nephritis), as well as acting as a mild diuretic. If you can, forage fresh nettles for this energising tea. If you encounter an abundance of them, gather extra to dry for later in the year.

Makes 1 x 300ml serving

15 nettle leaves or 1 teaspoon dried nettle leaves

2 sprigs of peppermint or 1 teaspoon dried mint

200ml freshly boiled water

If you are using fresh nettles, rinse them to remove any soil or grit. Place the fresh or dried leaves in a teapot along with the mint. Pour over the boiling water, followed by 100ml cold water. Steep for 10 minutes then strain into mugs. Drink warm or refrigerate and drink cold.

Scarborough fayre tea

With a quartet of healing herbs – rosemary for concentration, thyme to soothe respiratory issues, parsley for its iron content and sage to nourish a sore throat – this is a beautiful winter brew to stave off colds and bugs.

Makes 1 x 250ml serving

2 sprigs of rosemary

2 sprigs of thyme

3 sage leaves

1 large sprig of parsley

200ml freshly boiled water

Pile the fresh herbs into a teapot. Pour over the freshly boiled water and top up with 50ml cold water. Steep for 7 minutes then strain into a mug.

Holy basil tea

Also known as tulsi, holy basil is nutritive to the adrenal glands, making this tea helpful for those suffering from adrenal fatigue. It also helps reduce levels of cortisol, a stress hormone produced by the adrenal glands, making it useful for combatting anxiety and cortisol-driven weight gain.

Makes 1 x 250ml serving

1 tablespoon holy basil leaves

½ teaspoon chopped lemongrass or ginger, or ½ cinnamon stick

250ml boiled water

Infuse all the ingredients in boiling hot water in a teapot for 5 minutes.

Strain into tea cups and drink warm or chill and serve over ice.

Good digestion teas

Zen tea

There's plenty of digestive loveliness in this
recipe. Sip it slowly as it contains a powerhouse
of ingredients that the body needs to absorb slowly.

Makes 2 x 250ml servings

3 x 1cm slices fresh ginger

1 tablespoon dried
peppermint or 6 sprigs of
fresh peppermint

¼ teaspoon caraway seeds

¼ teaspoon fennel seeds

¼ teaspoon coriander seeds

1 star anise

500ml freshly boiled water

Add the herbs and spices to a teapot and pour over the
freshly boiled water. Steep for 5–10 minutes and strain
into mugs.

Tummy soother

Fennel is used widely in Ayurvedic medicine for digestive
issues. It can occasionally cause nausea so if it's a new
ingredient for you, start with a little and build up. Avoid
liquorice in cases of uncontrolled high blood pressure.

Makes 2 x 250ml servings

1 tablespoon dried peppermint

6 cloves

1 teaspoon fennel seeds

½ liquorice root

500ml freshly boiled water

Add the peppermint, cloves and fennel seeds to a teapot.
Crush or snap the liquorice a little. Pour over the freshly
boiled water. Steep for 5–10 minutes then strain into mugs.

Women's balance tea

This is a luxurious, calming, soothing tea to help ease fluctuations within a woman's monthly reproductive cycle. Sipping tea made with rose petals can help alleviate heavy bleeding. Here they're paired with saffron and raspberry leaves, which are both known to help relieve menstrual pain. The vanilla is there to sweeten and soothe. Shatavari is a species of asparagus which makes a wonderful tonic to help nourish the reproductive system – if you can find the powered root do include it (see page 92 for resources), although the tea is still as delicious and beneficial without it. Men enjoy this tea, too!

Makes 1 x 250ml serving

1 teaspoon dried raspberry leaves

1 tablespoon dried rose petals or buds

A pinch of saffron threads

2cm slice of vanilla pod (optional)

½ teaspoon shatavari root powder (optional)

300ml freshly boiled water

Put the raspberry leaves, rose petals, saffron, vanilla and shatavari (if using) into a teapot and pour over the freshly boiled water. Steep for 10 minutes then strain into a mug.

Vietnamese lemongrass tea

Lemongrass is brilliant for taming achy tummies. A mild astringent and antiseptic due to the lemonal compound contained in lemongrass, it's also great for soothing coughs and keeping colds and flu at bay.

Makes 2 x 250ml servings

4 lemongrass stems

1 thumb-sized piece of ginger

½–1 tablespoon coconut sugar or raw honey, to taste

Lime slices, to garnish (optional)

Bring 600ml water to a boil over high heat in a medium saucepan.

Bash and cut the lemongrass into thin shreds. Peel and julienne the ginger. Add both to the water and boil for 5 minutes.

Reduce the heat to low and simmer the tea for an additional 5 minutes. Sweeten to taste with the coconut sugar or honey.

Serve warm, or refrigerate and serve over ice, garnished with lime slices if you wish.

Tom yum tea

A brilliant cold-busting tea that tastes rather like Tom Yum soup. Take two to three times daily when you feel a cold coming on, but avoid drinking it late at night as the ginger and cayenne make this quite a stimulating tea.

Makes 1 x 200ml serving

1 lemon

1 garlic clove

2cm piece of fresh ginger

A pinch of cayenne pepper

200ml freshly boiled water

½–1 teaspoon raw honey or maple syrup

Strip the lemon zest using a vegetable peeler and put it into a mug. Squeeze in the juice (straining out the pips). Peel and grate or crush the garlic straight into the mug. Peel and grate in the ginger and add a pinch of cayenne pepper.

Pour over the freshly boiled water and steep for 5–10 minutes. Sweeten with honey or maple syrup to taste.

Armenian herbal tea

The Armenian highlands, located in the mountainous region between the Black and Caspian Seas, host pristine alpine habitats that produce an abundance of wild herbs. A blend of wild mountain thyme and linden flowers is widely sipped for both its flavour and nourishing qualities. Forage lime flowers in May or June, or buy them online.

Makes 1 x 250ml serving

6 sprigs of fresh thyme

1 teaspoon lime flowers

A strip of fresh orange zest (optional)

250ml freshly boiled water

Put the thyme, lime flowers and orange zest (if using) in a teapot and pour over the freshly boiled water. Steep for 5 minutes then strain into a mug.

Spice route teas

Saffron and cardamom tea

An elegant blend of spices and green tea, this brew also packs a health punch. Studies in India suggest that cardamom may be helpful in cases of colorectal cancer, while saffron is rich in crocin, a carotene that helps to ensure cells stay health.

Makes 1 x 250ml serving

4 cardamom pods

A pinch of saffron

2 teaspoon green tea leaves or 1 green tea bag

200ml freshly boiled water

Roughly crush the cardamom pods and put them in a teapot (both the green husks and the black seeds) with the saffron and tea leaves. Pour in the freshly boiled water and top up with 50ml cold water. Steep for 7 minutes then strain into a mug.

Spice C tea

Cumin is a wonderful aid for cleansing the small intestine, which plays an important role in digestion in terms of nutrient absorption. You may be eating the best food but if your ability to absorb and assimilate the nutrients is diminished, this will have a considerable impact on your health. Try this tea for one month in such cases.

Makes 1 x 250ml serving

1 teaspoon cumin seeds

½ cinnamon stick

2 teaspoon black tea leaves (or 1 black tea bag)

250ml freshly boiled water

Put the cumin, cinnamon and tea leaves into a teapot and pour over the freshly boiled water. Steep for 7 minutes, then strain into a mug.

Rosy ginger tea

Rose is a lovely medicine for your heart in terms of calming your emotions, while the ginger and star anise are great digestive soothers.

Makes 1 x 250ml serving

3cm piece of fresh ginger, peeled and roughly chopped

1 tablespoon rose petals or buds

1 star anise

250ml freshly boiled water

Put the ginger, rose petals or buds and star anise into a teapot and pour over the freshly boiled water. Steep for 10 minutes then strain into a mug.

Afghan pink chai

This intriguing, traditional Afghan drink, also known as Qaimaq or Sheer chai, is often served at celebrations to toast good health. The addition of bicarbonate of soda is what magically turns the green tea-based drink pink. Traditional recipes use condensed milk which exaggerates the colour, but it's laden with fat and sugar so I've used a healthier alternative and added a little beetroot juice to further the effect. Bicarbonate is helpful for the acid/alkali balance in the body.

Serves 2

1 tablespoon loose leaf green tea or green tea bag

⅛ teaspoon bicarbonate of soda

500ml raw cow's milk or almond milk

Roughly crushed seeds from 6 cardamom pods

1 cinnamon stick

10 cloves

1 teaspoon beetroot juice or powdered beetroot (optional)

1–2 teaspoon raw honey or coconut palm sugar, to taste (optional)

Place everything, apart from the beetroot juice or honey, into a saucepan. Bring to a rapid boil for 1 minute.

Turn off the heat and let it steep for 15 minutes. It should be a pale shade of pink. For added blush, whisk in a little beetroot juice or powdered beetroot, if you like.

Strain the spices from the drink and sweeten to taste. Serve warm.

Vanilla and nutmeg matcha latte

Unlike other green teas – where you steep the leaves and then strain them – with this you're actually consuming dried and powdered leaves. Thus, matcha is packed with antioxidants and it offers a sustained energy boost. It's a great alternative to coffee, as it gives you a caffeine buzz without the subsequent crash.

Makes 1 x 250ml serving

250ml almond milk

Drop of vanilla extract (less than ⅛ tsp) or a small scraping of vanilla seeds (less than ¼ pod)

A pinch of freshly grated nutmeg

1 teaspoon matcha powder

½–1 teaspoon raw honey or maple syrup

Gently warm the milk with the vanilla and nutmeg. Increase the heat and bring to a soft, rolling boil, then remove from the heat.

Whisk in the matcha powder until frothy. Sweeten to taste with honey or maple syrup.

Serve warm or, in summer, just whisk everything together and serve cold.

Drinks

Golden lassi

The anti-inflammatory action of turmeric, combined with mineral-rich bananas or mango, make this a good lassi to choose for muscle recovery after a workout.

Makes 2 x 300ml servings

1 large thumb-sized piece of turmeric or 1 teaspoon ground turmeric

2 bananas or 1 smallish ripe mango

400ml natural yogurt or dairy kefir

Peel the turmeric and place in a blender or food-processor.

Peel the bananas or peel and cut the flesh from the stone of the mango. Add the fruit to blender or food-processor, along with the yogurt or kefir, and blend until smooth. Trickle in a little water to thin, if needed. Drink straight away or chill and drink within 24 hours.

Frothy ayran

Originating from Turkey, this frothy yogurt drink is made during the summer months as it can help to hydrate you, and the addition of salt helps replace natural salts lost through sweating. It's traditionally taken as an antidote to spicy foods, so serve it up to cool down your favourite spicy dishes.

Makes 2 x 250ml servings

150g full-fat natural yogurt

A pinch of sea salt

350ml sparkling water

Ice and fresh or dried mint, to serve

Put the yogurt and salt in a blender or large bowl and blend or whisk in the sparkling water little by little, until frothy and well mixed. Pour into glasses with ice and garnish with a few sprigs of fresh mint or a sprinkling of dried mint.

Nut, seed and grain milks

Ok, so technically these are not milk, but all are brilliant substitutes. You can blend pretty much any seed, nut or grain with water, strain, and magically it produces a brilliant milk alternative. Plant-based milks are easier to digest and contain a wide array of nutrients, especially if you use a mix of different nuts, seeds and grains.

Basics

Makes 400ml

100g nuts, seeds or grains

1–2 pitted dates (optional)

Cover the nuts or seeds with water and soak in the fridge overnight or for 12 hours (only soak the pinhead variety of oats). To sweeten, add 1 or 2 pitted dates before soaking.

Once soaked, drain and rinse. Blend with four times the volume of water, so blend 100g of nuts, seeds or grains, with 400ml filtered or mineral water. Strain, squeezing out any liquid. Store in the fridge for up to 5 days.

Milk combos

Almond and mixed seed milk Sunflower, sesame and pumpkin seeds are delicious blended with almonds and add nutritional benefits. Blend 50/50 almonds and seeds, either one type or a mix.

Hemp seed milk Delicious on its own or 50/50 with almonds or cashews. Also lovely blended with a date or two, a drop of vanilla and 1 teaspoon ground cinnamon.

Oat milk Perfect in banana-based smoothies, or warm with honey and nutmeg for a soothing bedtime drink.

Cashew milk This is the thickest, creamiest and most milk-like of all and is lovely cold with a dusting of cinnamon.

Hazelnut milk This is one of my favourite milks and is delicious in the Chicory Chai on page 50 or in the Aztec Hot Chocolate on page 79.

Coconut milk

Fresh coconut milk is rich in antioxidants and will give your immune system a boost. It also acts as a muscle relaxant, due to its high mineral content, and is antibacterial. Half the fat found in coconut is called lauric acid, which the body converts to monolaurin that acts to destroy viruses and gram-negative bacteria. The medium-chain fatty acids also found in coconut oil and milk have many health benefits as they are easily digested and go straight to the liver to be used for energy.

Makes 750ml

1 coconut

Approx. 750ml filtered or mineral water

Crack your coconut open. A great tip is to wrap it in a clean tea towel or muslin then set it in a metal bowl and bash it with a mallet or hammer. Then use the cloth to strain the water away from the coconut into the bowl to use later.

Pry the flesh from the shell using a knife and roughly chop – it's fine to leave on the brown skin. Put the flesh into a food-processor or blender and start blending it, adding the coconut water and then filtered or mineral water, a little at a time, until the coconut flesh is as fine as desiccated coconut and the liquid is thick and creamy. Add more or less water, depending on the size of your coconut and how thick and creamy you want it.

Strain the coconut milk using a piece of muslin or a fine mesh sieve. Reserve the pulp for use in salads, or dry it to make your own desiccated coconut.

Store in the fridge for 2–3 days, or freeze for up to 6 months. Defrost in the fridge.

Golden chai

Makes 1 x 250ml serving

250ml almond milk

2 small or 1 large turmeric root, peeled and roughly chopped

Seeds from 2 cardamom pods

A pinch of freshly ground pepper

1 teaspoon coconut oil

1 teaspoon raw honey or maple syrup, to taste

Turmeric has been widely researched and the compound curcumin is believed to provide a plethora of benefits, including modulation of gene expression, reduction of inflammation, protection against liver damage, enhanced wound healing and suppression of tumour formation. It also has an extremely safe profile so is a wonderful addition to anyone's daily diet.

Blend the almond milk with the turmeric, cardamom, pepper and coconut oil. Sweeten with honey or maple syrup to taste. Drink cold or warm.

If you want to increase the quantities and make a large batch to drink throughout the week, it will kept nicely in the fridge for 4–5 days.

Ruby latte

Makes 1 x 250ml serving

250ml almond or coconut milk

2 tablespoons beetroot juice or 1 tablespoon beetroot powder

Pinch of ground cinnamon

¼ teaspoon vanilla (seeds or extract)

1cm slice of fresh ginger

Ground seeds from 2 cardamom pods (optional)

This is part of a growing range of superfood lattes and features beetroot, a plant-based milk and a blend of spice. It's hugely satisfying and, unlike coffee, will lower blood pressure.

Warm the milk with the beetroot juice or powder and spices. Whisk until frothy and warmed through. Serve straight away, or make up the mixture the night before, store in a jam jar and warm up in the morning.

Butter-froth coffee

Makes 2 x 200ml servings

4 tablespoons freshly ground organic coffee beans

400ml freshly boiled water

50ml cold water

2 tablespoons grass-fed butter or ghee

2 tablespoons coconut oil (or Bulletproof Brain Octane Oil, available online)

This is like a coffee version of butter beer. If you are a coffee-lover, try this as a clean and nutritious alternative; the addition of butter and coconut oil make it much easier on insulin and adrenal responses. Go easy on caffeine if you have over-active adrenals or suffer from panic attacks.

Brew the coffee in a filter or a cafetière with the mix of hot and cold water. If using a cafetière, steep for 5 minutes before pressing.

Blend the coffee with the butter or ghee and the oil for 5 minutes, or until frothy. Drink straight away

Aztec hot chocolate

Makes 2 x 150ml servings

4 tablespoons freshly grated 100% raw chocolate (cacao), or raw cocoa powder

½ teaspoon vanilla extract or the seeds scraped from ½ a vanilla pod

½ teaspoon ground cinnamon

A pinch of chilli powder

A pinch of ground Szechuan pepper (optional)

300ml boiling water or warm milk (any kind)

1–2 tablespoons raw honey or maple syrup, to taste

Raw cacao is rich in minerals, especially magnesium and potassium. The buzz from the heat of the chilli and pepper aids the circulation. The cinnamon also helps to stimulate blood flow to cold extremities, so wrap your hands around a hot mug of goodness. Even the smell of the vanilla is enough to imbue the spirit with a lift! Vanilla is also showing promise for alleviating depression.

Spoon the chocolate, vanilla, cinnamon, chilli and Szechuan pepper (if using) into a saucepan. Slowly whisk in the water or milk until the mixture is dark, thick and a little frothy. Gently boil, whisking often, until thickened. Sweeten with honey or maple syrup to taste.

Brown rice horchata

This drink is a good option ahead of any endurance event such as a marathon. It is rich in carbohydrates and minerals from the dates as well as the blood-sugar-balancing effects of cinnamon, so taking it daily in the week leading up to the event can be helpful. Add 2 teaspoons of hemp seed protein to turn it into a breakfast packed with nutrients.

Makes 2 x 250ml servings

100g organic brown rice, rinsed*

300g almond or raw cow's milk

Seeds from ½ vanilla pod or 1 teaspoon extract

½ teaspoon ground cinnamon, plus more for garnish

A pinch of sea salt

1–2 tablespoons maple syrup

Ice, 1 cinnamon stick and a pinch of ground cinnamon, to garnish (optional)

I used medium-grain brown rice, but short- and long-grain should work too. Use white rice instead if you like.

Place the rice and 300ml water into a lidded container. Cover and refrigerate overnight.

Transfer the rice and water to a blender and process until smooth. Using a muslin cloth or fine sieve, strain the mixture, making sure to extract as much liquid as possible.

Return the liquid back to the blender and add the almond or raw cow's milk, vanilla, cinnamon and salt. Process until frothy then whizz in 1 tablespoon of maple syrup. Taste and adjust the sweetness if necessary.

Serve over ice and garnish with a cinnamon stick and a light dusting of ground cinnamon, if you like.

Horchata will keep for 4–5 days in the fridge. Give it a quick stir before serving as it has a tendency to separate.

Kombucha

This tangy, refreshing drink is made with a scoby, which stands for 'symbiotic colony of bacteria and yeast'. It's a fermented drink and helpful for creating a harmonious internal microbiome – your gut flora – which is pivotal to overall health. Go easy if you're not used to fermented food and drink. Start slowly and build up, drinking occasionally and tuning into its effects.

Makes 1 litre or 4 x 250ml servings

4 tablespoons whole tea leaves or 3 tea bags*

85g unrefined (raw if possible) caster sugar

1 litre freshly boiled water

1 kombucha scoby (see page 92)

4 tablespoons kombucha or raw apple cider vinegar

* You can use any kind of tea so long as it has tannins, which provide food to keep the scoby going. Try white, green, oolong, earl grey or a scented tea – jasmine pearls from Jing Tea is my favourite. You can also experiment with spices: add your favourite chai spices to a batch of black or oolong tea kombucha for a unique brew.

Add the tea leaves and sugar to a sterilised, heatproof 1.5 litre glass jar. Let the water cool a little, then add to the jar. Stir to help dissolve the sugar, and let it steep for 1 hour.

Strain the mixture and return it to the container along with the kombucha scoby. Cover the jar with a piece of muslin or a thin, clean tea-towel. Secure with string or a rubber band and leave to ferment for 1–2 weeks. Taste after a week; you're aiming for a flavour that's a little yeasty but also midly tangy, a little like cider vinegar. The longer you ferment it, the sourer and less sweet it will taste.

Once brewed, pour into bottles and store in the fridge for up to 6 weeks.

After pouring your brew into bottles, store your scoby in a container at room temperature with at 4 tablespoons of kombucha. It will keep for several weeks between brews.

FIZZY HANGOVER HELP
Brew kombucha as above but add a few slices of fresh ginger with the tea, or add 1 teaspoon freshly grated ginger to 250ml kombucha. Infuse for 10 minutes, strain, then whisk in 1 teaspoon of vitamin C-rich Camu Camu powder. It tastes – and fizzes – similarly to Berocca, and gives you a wonderful vitamin boost.

Hibiscus cooler

Also known as 'Agua de Jamaica', this popular drink is sold across Mexico, where an abundance of hibiscus plants line the roads. Hibiscus helps to ease coughs and colds and soothe sore throats. It's also useful for treating cystitis, helping menstruation pain and lowering blood pressure. When using for therapeutic purposes, aim to drink two or three cups daily for acute conditions.

Makes 1 litre or 4 x 250ml servings

5 tablespoons dried hibiscus flowers

1 litre freshly boiled water

2–4 tablespoons raw honey or maple syrup

1 lime, juiced

Put the hibiscus flowers in a heatproof jug or container. Let the boiling water cool slightly, then add to the jug with 2 tablespoons of honey or maple syrup. Infuse for at least an hour, or preferably overnight, in the fridge.

Strain the flowers out. Add more sweetener and lime juice, to taste. Drink cold.

Tepache

A popular fermented beverage in Mexico that's made from the peel and the rind of pineapples, sweetened with piloncillo or brown sugar, seasoned with cinnamon and served cold. Though fermented for several days, the drink only contains a small amount of alcohol.

Makes 4 x 250ml servings

1 pineapple, peel and rind

100g brown sugar or Mexican Piloncillo sugar

1 cinnamon stick

3 cloves

1 litre filtered or mineral water

Rinse the pineapple peel and finely chop. Place in a 1.5-litre jar then add the sugar, spices and water. Cover with a piece of muslin or a clean tea-towel and secure with string. Set in a dark, cool place to ferment for 24 hours.

Spoon off any white foam that has formed on the top. Cover again and leave for a further 24–36 hours. Don't let it ferment longer or you'll end up with pineapple vinegar.

Strain and pour into sterilised bottles or serve straight away. Store in the fridge for up to 1 week.

Blood orange ginger beer

Making ginger beer is surprisingly easy and extremely satisfying.
It takes about a week to ferment, and 5 minutes hands-on attention
a day. You can substitute any seasonal fruit (rhubarb is amazing),
or experiment with herbs and spices such as star anise, cinnamon
or cardamom. Use organic ginger because you are leaving the skin
on – this houses all of the lovely bacteria and yeasts.

Makes 1 litre

1 whole organic fresh ginger
root, unpeeled (approx.
12cm in length)

6 teaspoons unrefined caster
sugar, plus 175g

5 blood oranges

In a 500ml jar mix 1 tablespoon grated ginger, 1 teaspoon
sugar and 3 tablespoons water. Cover with a piece of
muslin or a clean tea-towel and leave to ferment in a dark,
cool place for 24 hours, shaking it a couple of times.

After 24 hours, stir in 1 tablespoon grated ginger,
1 teaspoon sugar and 2 tablespoons water. Repeat daily
for five days; you should start to see it fizz a little. This is
your 'ginger bug'.

On the sixth day, strip the zest of 2 oranges using a vegetable
peeler. In a saucepan, combine the zest with the juice from
all of the oranges and enough filtered or mineral water to
bring the mix up to 1 litre in total. Add the 175g of sugar.
Simmer for 15 minutes, or until the sugar has dissolved.

Cool completely then pour into a 1.5 litre lidded jar. Add
half the ginger bug, or to taste. Cover with a piece of
muslin, secured with a rubber band, and store in a dark
place. Stir once or twice daily. Top up the remainder of the
ginger bug up for future batches and store in the fridge.

Variation
Turmeric soda:
replace the ginger with
6 large thumbs of fresh
organic turmeric and the
blood oranges with zest
and juice of 2 lemons.

Taste the ginger beer daily, it will continue to ferment and
become less sweet. Once to your liking – generally 3–4 days
– strain out the zest and pour into sterilised bottles. Let
the bottles sit at room temperature for a day or two, then
refrigerate.

You may need to 'burp' your bottles once or twice
by opening then resealing them. This will release the
pressure and prevent your bottles from exploding. Once
refrigerated, drink within 2 weeks.

Jun tea

Thought to have originated in northern China and Tibet, Jun is a probiotic drink made with raw honey and green tea. It's a light, effervescent, sweet and slightly sour alternative to Kombucha. If you're avoiding sugar, you may prefer it.

Makes 4 x 250ml servings

1 litre filtered or mineral water

1 tablespoon loose-leaf green tea (any variety)

75g raw honey

1 jun scoby (available to order online, see page 92 for suppliers)

75ml Jun Tea from previous batch (comes with your scoby for your first brew)

Bring 1 litre of water to the boil in a saucepan and add the tea leaves, then remove from the heat. Steep for 30 minutes then strain. Whisk in the honey until it dissolves.

Pour into a sterilised 2.5-litre jar and add the Jun scoby and tea from a previous batch. Cover the jar with a piece of muslin or a clean tea-towel and secure with string or a rubber band. Place the jar in a cool, dark place and sit it on a plate or dish to catch any liquid that may bubble over.

Taste after 3 days. It should smell a little sweet and faintly sour. If you like the taste, bottle it up and make a new batch (see page 82 for looking after your scoby) or leave it for a few more days. The longer you ferment it, the more sour it will become.

Bottle the jun tea in sterilised bottles then leave on the side, at room temperature, for 2 more days to get a little bubbly. Store in the fridge until ready to drink. It will keep for 6 weeks or more.

Rye kvass

This traditional Slavic and Baltic brew is a healthy substitute for beer and a quick homebrew with a very low alcohol content. It is nutritious, cooling and energising, as well as an excellent digestive tonic. It's also rich in iron with molasses, which acts as an overall blood builder.

Makes 1 litre

100g stale 100% rye sourdough

2 tablespoons molasses

2 tablespoons raisins, dried sour cherries or 100g fresh blackberries

1 tablespoon active sourdough starter (shop bought or fresh*)

1.5 litres filtered or mineral water

Whisk 100g strong bread flour with 100ml warm water in a clean jar. Cover with a cloth and leave in a warm place for 1 day, stirring occasionally. Feed the mix with 100g flour and 100ml cold water. When it bubbles and rises, it's ready to use.

Cut the bread into 2cm cubes. Ensure it is really dry. If not, place in a low oven until fully dry but not burnt or toasted.

Put all the ingredients into a large jar (or evenly divide between two jars), leaving at least 5cm at the top. Cover with a piece of muslin or a clean tea-towel and set in a shaded spot away from direct sunlight. Leave to ferment for 2–4 days, or until it becomes tangy and beer like. You should also see bubbles forming.

When you decide that the kvass is ready, put it in the fridge for a few hours, or overnight. As it cools down, all the lees and bread solids will sink to the bottom of the jar. Strain the kvass carefully through muslin, trying not to disturb the sediment at the bottom, and pour into sterilised bottles. Kvass can be safely stored in the fridge for up to a week.

Moroccan mull

This beautiful, aromatic drink is brimming with antioxidants, heart-healthy pomegranate and warming spices, and is a brilliant alternative to mulled wine during the festive period. Every time I offer guests a choice between this and mulled red wine, they're always swayed toward this version.

Makes 4 x 250ml servings

1 litre pomegranate juice

1 tablespoon rose petals or 2 teaspoons rose water

8 cardamom pods, crushed

2 star anise

2 cinnamon sticks

12 cloves

2 clementines

Put all the ingredients into a large saucepan and simmer for 15 minutes. Strain into heatproof glasses. For a richer flavour, steep the mixture in the fridge overnight and then warm before serving.

My little black book

Get all you need to make the recipes throughout this book with these wonderful suppliers.

Jing Tea – one of the best ranges of loose leaf and herbal teas
www.jingtea.com

Neal's Yard – dried herbs and flowers for making teas and tonics
www.nealsyardremedies.com

G. Baldwin & Co. – another brilliant source for dried herbs for making your own tea blends
www.baldwins.co.uk

Food for All – extensive range of herbs for making teas and tonics
www.foodforall.co.uk

Happy Kombucha – for kombucha scoby and kefir grains
www.happykombucha.co.uk

Kombucha Kamp – for jun tea scoby
https://store.kombuchakamp.com/jun-culture

Aconbury Sprouts – for organic wheatgrass kits
www.wheatgrass-uk.com

Indigo Herbs – for brahmi, shatavari, beetroot and camu camupowders
www.indigo-herbs.co.uk

Ciara Jean Roberts – for nutritional guidance
www.whollyaligned.com

Drinks for...

Allergies and hay fever: *Lemon, lavender and peppermint shot*

Anti-aging: *White tea, Green tea, Olive leaf tea, Citrus wake-up calls, Saffron and cardamom tea*

Arthritis: *Everyday health tonic, Golden chai, Turmeric shots, Olive leaf tea, Elderflower and lemon tea*

Bedtime: *Cosy bedtime tea, Sweet dreams tea*

Blood pressure and circulation: *Lime and cayenne pepper shot, Aztec hot chocolate, Moroccan mull*

Breakfast: *Brain booster, Tropical detox smoothie, Golden chai, Golden lassi, Brown rice horchata*

Children: *Rosehip syrup, Golden lassi, Brown rice horchata, Hibiscus tea*

Coffee addicts: *Brain booster, Chicory chai, Butter-froth coffee*

Coughs and sore throats: *Cough tonic, Bee balm vinegar, Elderflower vinegar, Elderflower and lemon tea*

Detoxing: *Dandelion and burdock cordial, Spiced dandelion tea, Celery and coriander juice, Wheatgrass and gooseberry juice, Charcoal shot, Nettle and mint tea*

Digestion: *Zen tea, Mint vinegar, Puerh tea, Spice c tea, Rosy ginger tea*

Energy: *Vanilla and nutmeg matcha latte, Chlorella and coconut water, Jamu kunyit, Turmeric shots, Coconut milk*

Fighting colds: *Everyday health tonic, Garlic and lemon elixir, Thyme vinegar, Oregano vinegar, Tom yum tea*

Focus and concentration: *Brain booster, Rosemary vinegar, Grasshopper tea*

Gut Health (pro- and pre-biotic): *Water kefir, Milk kefir, Chicory chai, Sunflower seed milk, kombucha, Jun tea, Rye kvass*

Hangovers: *Wheatgrass and gooseberry juice, Fizzy hangover help*

Headaches and migraines: *Seasonal ginger shots, Lemon, lavender and peppermint shot*

Immune boosting: *Elderberry syrup with echinacea, Rosehip syrup, Scarborough fayre tea*

Iron boosting: *Nettle tonic, Beetroot kvass, Apple and parsley juice*

Menstrual cramps: *Lemon verbena and calendula tea, Women's balance tea, hibiscus tea*

Parasites: *Celery and coriander juice, Tropical detox smoothie, Pumpkin seed milk*

Relaxation and reducing anxiety: *Jasmine tea, Holy basil tea, Sweet dreams tea*

Upset tummies: *Seasonal ginger shots, Aloe cooler, Vietnamese lemongrass tea, Tummy soother*

Index

Acknowledgements

Writing this book has made me realise just how much of my day is devoted to brewing and sipping things. It's been brilliant to have the opportunity to dote on my favourite infusions and bind them all together in this wonderful little tome.

Huge thanks to Judith Hannah and Kyle Cathie for thinking of me for this project. You're the of the wisest owls in the publishing world and it's been delightful working with you again. And, to Rebecca Sullivan for reconnecting us.

To the lovely Hannah Coughlin, thank you for pulling everything together, guiding the shoots, letting me slip in extra recipes at the umpteenth hour, and for really shaping this book.

This book would not be as beautiful and inspiring without photographer Ali Allen's stunning images, and Lucy Gowans' design skills. I could just pour over the gorgeous pages all day.

Eternal thanks to Edward Eisler from Jing Tea for opening the door to the wonderful world of tea. Your teas really are the finest and drinking them brightens my days. Enormous gratitude to Sally Gurteen for further adding to my tea knowledge.

Thank you to Sara Haglund for gifting me my first Scoby, which kickstarted many kombucha brewing adventures. To my friends and family, for trying all my weird and wonderful brews.

Last but not least, to Ciara Jean Roberts, who I've been seeing as a nutritional therapist for the past few years. You have poured a vast wealth of knowledge into this book. You have also taught me (and hopefully those of you who have bought this book) that simple, joyful and delicious routines woven into your day can really make a dramatic difference to how you feel.